Silver Strings Of Midnight

Poetry of Longing, Light and Letting go

Shikha Arya

Made with ❤ on the BookLeaf Publishing Platform
www.bookleafpub.in
www.bookleafpub.com

Dedication

To my younger brother—my strongest ally, best buddy, and constant beacon of hope in the darkest hours. From growing up together to supporting one another's development, we have experienced love, grief, laughter, and life lessons that have moulded us. Your faith in me has been my rock, your words have been my solace, and your presence has been my greatest blessing through all the highs and lows. You have helped me get back up when I fell, encouraged me when I faltered, and reminded me that aspirations should be pursued rather than avoided. I dedicate this book to you because you always remind me that love and support endure no matter how far apart we are from one another. It examines the beauty and suffering of human connections —of clinging to, letting go, and finding meaning in the voids between.

Preface

21 Strings of Midnight is a collection of moments—quiet reflections woven from thoughts, emotions, and the subtle ties between myself and the world around me. Each poem is a thread, drawn from observations, feelings, and connections that lingered long after the day had ended. Midnight became a space for clarity—a time when the world felt still enough to hear my inner voice take shape in words. These 21 pieces came together not with intention but with necessity. They are traces of becoming, fragments of realisation, and gentle reminders of how much can be said in silence. If you're holding this book, thank you. I hope something within these pages speaks to your own experiences or brings you closer to understanding your own strings of midnight.

Acknowledgements

This book would not have been possible without the love, presence, and quiet encouragement of those who supported me along the way. I am deeply grateful to BookLeaf Publishing for giving *21 Strings of Midnight* a place in the world and for believing in this collection from the beginning. To my parents, thank you for your endless support, patience, and love—you have been the foundation beneath every word I write, and I carry your strength with me always. To the people who stood by me, whether with words or simply with their presence, your energy and kindness helped shape these poems more than you know. And to the stillness of midnight, where these thoughts found space to become poetry, thank you. This book is for anyone who has ever felt something deeply and tried to find the right words for it —I hope these pages offer you a gentle reflection of your own journey.

1. Chandelier

You are the chandelier of my home—
 a radiant centre,
 brightest of every light.
Most chandeliers grace perfect walls,
 smooth, unbroken.
 But you chose mine—
 cracked, fragile,
 barely holding their shape.
Your light seeps into each fissure,
 turning scars into prisms,
 fractures into brilliance.
Between us, only one thread holds.
 Delicate, unbreakable—
 enough to keep you near
 as you make this brokenness gleam.

2. A Shape-Shifter

I am a shape-shifter,
 slipping between shadows and sun,
 the weathered chair that settles
 into the corner of any room.
Some call me a chameleon,
 their words heavy with accusation—
 as if blending were a betrayal.
 But this is not shielding.
 This is the art of becoming:
The laughter of the joker,
 the wisdom of the sage.
 A vintage heel, cracked and rare,
 too old for now, too new for then.
 I am many things—
 and I am whole.

3. Joker

You made me a joker,
laughter pulling threads from my soul,
unravelling the seams of who I am.
Even in the numbness, I feel it—
every joke's echo ricocheting inside me,
every laugh tugging me further from myself.
Still, deep below the waves,
a crystal jellyfish pulses—
fragile, glowing, alive.
Perhaps hope lives there,
faint, like light through water,
refusing to drown.

4. Party

You hosted a party and invited me.
The room shimmered with laughter,
glasses clinking,
a sea of familiar faces.
But I stood in the corner,
a shadow dissolving into the walls,
my reflection glaring back,
too sharp to ignore.
You wanted me to measure myself
against the room—
to see my worth through your eyes.
But ice doesn't last.
It cracks, splinters, and melts.
When I walked out,
I knew not one of you could afford me.
Not even you.

5. The Fire That I Carry

5

The fire in my heart grows,
 its vines unfurling, reaching for you,
 their heat grazing your skin,
 twisting into your soul.
Do you feel it—
 this hunger,
 this heat that climbs?
Hold it, if you dare.
 Let it thread through your veins,
 ignite the hidden corners of you.
Will it devour us both,
 or will we blaze together,
 burning the world to its bones,
 leaving only embers—
 a memory of what we were?

6. A Beast

6

There's a beast within everyone.
 Some call it darkness,
 some call it fire.
 For some, it is a torch,
 while others run from its flames.
 To some, it is an escape,
 a door left open in the night.
Then why do we call it evil,
 when it can also be a triumph?

7. To God, with anger

I am enraged with You.
It feels like nothing matters, no matter what I do.
How much more can I give?
How good can I be?
I have begun to question myself—
What did I do to deserve Your silence?
You lift those who cast others aside,
bless the hands that break instead of build.
Yet here I stand—unheard, unseen—
my prayers dissolving into nothing.
I no longer know who to trust,
or even who I am.
You have woven the world in disguise.
I came as myself to a costume party,
yet still, You favour the ones in masks.
I feel like a hostage in my own cage—
maybe that's the only way I know how to survive.
And still, You advocate for them.
And still, I have nowhere else to go.

8. Mirror Maze

It's like I'm lost in a mirror maze,
 but every reflection is a stranger.
 I no longer recognize myself—
 versions of me stare back,
 their eyes shifting, uncertain,
 their faces warping like water.
 I can't say who to trust.
From a distance, every mirror tells a story,
 a canvas of emotions,
 painted with my flesh, my tears.
 They whisper doubts in voices I almost know,
 distorted echoes of who I used to be.
Sometimes, I want to shatter them all,
 let the glass splinter like the pieces of me.
 But the stones—their words, their judgment—
 built this maze around me,
 trapping my emotions behind cold reflections.
Maybe it's all inside my head.
 Or maybe... I am the mirror.

9. Shades of You

You paint my world with hues of laughter and light,
your laughter a palette that brightens the night.
In the mirror of moments, I see our reflections,
layered in memories, vivid connections.
With each brushstroke of your voice, I find my muse,
as we dance through the spectrum, boldly choose.
Together we blend in harmonious flight,
creating a canvas where the shadows take delight.
With you, love blossoms like a radiant bloom,
filling the corners of my heart's crowded room.

10. Seeds

I came to your land with hope in my eyes,
  seeds in my hands—an offering of love.
  These seeds were meant to bloom into flowers
  too rare for anyone to claim.
But you cast me out, stole my light,
  left me rootless in foreign soil.
  Now, I am too afraid to wander,
  too weary to plant again.

11. Time Machine

I built a time machine
that takes me to the past.
Through its window, I see myself—
radiant, unshaken, envied.
My blooming eyes once burned in sight,
too bright for them to bear.
Now I understand their envy,
but visiting my past is freezing my present.
So I've built another time machine—
this time, it moves forward,
showing me only the brightest possibilities.
Not just content, but truly happy.

12. Crownless, Not Worthless

If they take your crown, forge your own,
gold from fire, steel from stone.
Wear it high when shadows creep,
a throne is hers who dares to keep.
No army needed, no chorus sung,
a queen is crowned by her own tongue.
Let confidence shine, unchained, untamed,
jewels of fire that can't be claimed.
And when they whisper, doubt, or scheme,
stand tall—outlive their fleeting dream.
For time itself will come to see,
the world must bow—you are the queen.

With every step, let courage bloom,
shatter the silence, dispel the gloom.
Your voice, a river, strong and clear,
carving its path through doubt and fear.
With wisdom woven in each breath,
defy the odds, embrace your breadth.
In the theater of life, take your place,
a sovereign soul with boundless grace.
And when the stars align and call,
know in your spirit, you stand tall.

13. Gifts of a Rainbow

I'll paint a rainbow on your heart,
so life will never dull or darken.
Let these colors shape your days—
their light will never fade away.

Yellow, the strength of the shining sun,
a fire that never dims nor falls.
Green, like grass, will keep you grounded,
steady, rooted through it all.

Blue, an endless sky of thought,
boundless dreams, no walls, no chains.
Red, the rose—so soft, so fragile,
beauty held, yet love leaves stains.

Lavender, a jewel to crown you,
calm and pure, a royal hue.
These are the gifts I leave behind—
a rainbow, bright and made for you.

Orange whispers of warmth and hope,
igniting passions with its glow.
Violet sings of mysteries,
each note a secret only we know.

Each brushstroke blends in harmony,
a canvas rich with love's embrace.
Together, they will guide your way—
a tapestry time cannot erase.

14. Seekers

We are all seekers in this world.
Some search for survival,
some for love, honesty, grace.
Others chase fortune, wealth—
a thirst unquenched, a restless race.
Yet little do they come to see,
all they seek is near, inside.
No need to wander, beg, or plead—
just open your eyes, observe, abide.

In quiet moments, wisdom waits,
in whispered winds, the heart elates.
The laughter shared, the tears that blend,
in simple joys, our paths transcend.
The light we crave, in shadows cast,
is found in stillness, unsurpassed.
So pause a while, let silence speak,
in the depths of peace, our souls shall seek.

15. My Heart

I have always wondered—
 how much can it take?
 The love it pours,
 the sorrow it swallows,
 the suffering it silently bears.
 The fears it locks away.
How much can this little heart bury?
 Distant memories, golden days,
 the moments I would relive—
 even in the afterlife,
 even beyond time.
But memories pull me deeper,
 into an endless hollow,
 where the past plays again and again.
And here I fall asleep once more...

16. Pearl

I am no pearl
 for you to find—
  rare, hard, confined.
 I am no ornament to adorn you.
I am the ocean—deep, untamed,
 a thousand lives within my name.
 I shift, I rise, I fall, I roar,
 I am more than you ever saw before.
I exist in shades you fail to see,
 deeper than you know,
 shallower than you think.
 I can take any shape.
The sun and moon are my kin,
 rising and falling in me.
 I am the voice that soothes your soul,
 the breeze that sets your spirit free.

17. When the Night is Dark

When the night is dark,
I'll sing you to sleep.
I'll hold you close when nightmares call,
when shadows start to creep.
You can cling to me tighter,
let my warmth keep you safe.
I'll whisper you stories—
of what was, and what we dream.
And as the stars fade into dawn,
I'll still be here, holding on.
Through the gentle sighs of morning light,
our fears will dissolve like mist in flight.
With each golden ray that breaks the night,
I'll guard your heart till all feels right.

18. My Beloved, Come Home

My beloved, come home safely.
I want to run barefoot with you
through lavender fields again.
I still feel your warmth on cold nights.
Our children are growing,
but they need their father's voice, not just his stories.
I know you're fighting for the nation,
but must war always steal our time?
I'm tired of hiding behind the curtains—
I want to see the light.
Still, I wait for endless daylight,
for wind in our hair,
for love without fear.
Let the sun break through this shadow,
bring laughter back to our door,
as we gather 'round the table,
with tales of hope, not of war.
Hold me close and whisper softly,
as the world outside stands still—
we'll find our peace among the quiet,
as love ignites the heart's true will.

19. If They Cut Your Wings

If they cut your wings,
I'll stitch them anew.
I'll clash with God for rain
on the desert of you.
I'll bury my wishes
so yours may rise.
I'll be the roots
that hold you to life,
tangled and steadfast,
defying the knife.
In shadows, I'll whisper,
beneath the moon's glow,
tender spells woven,
to help you to grow.

20. The Tree of Life

Your life is like a tree,
each leaf holding a memory,
rooted deep within your soul.
Life is all about letting go and holding on—
with every fallen leaf, you leave something behind:
some beautiful, some bittersweet,
some you'd rather forget.
Yet some things cling to you,
like stubborn leaves that refuse to fall.
And just as leaves remind us
that trees are alive and breathing,
so too does light and shadow shape our days.
For a life without both good and evil
would question its very essence.
But if you hold onto kindness,
nurture the good within,
the universe will reward you—with fruit.
In the quiet moments, listen,
for whispers of the past still echo
in the rustle of your branches,
as the seasons weave their tapestry—
a cycle of growth and decay,
reminding you that even in the depths of winter,

new buds are waiting, dormant yet alive,
to burst forth when the world is ready.

21. Lightning

Everybody fears me now.
I have become lightning—
a blaze in the storm,
a roar in the void.
I turn darkness into beauty,
yet mankind trembles at my voice.
I am seen. I am heard.
Only the heights embrace me.
In shadows, my whispers linger,
a dance of dread and awe,
as I carve the silence with sparks,
my fury a painter's brush.
They shield their eyes from my glow,
but in their hearts, they know,
I am the storm they cannot tame,
the fire that fuels their flame.

www.ingramcontent.com/pod-product-compliance
Lightning Source LLC
LaVergne TN
LVHW010851200726
843508LV00012B/2851